STRANGE BUT TRUE!

FOOTBALL

Paul Mason

W
FRANKLIN WATTS
LONDON • SYDNEY

Franklin Watts
Published in Great Britain in 2018
by The Watts Publishing Group
Copyright © The Watts Publishing Group, 2017
All rights reserved.

Credits
Series Editors: Paul Mason and Sarah Peutrill
Series Designer: Matt Lilly

ISBN 978 1 4451 5721 4

Printed in China

FSC
www.fsc.org
MIX
Paper from
responsible sources
FSC® C104740

Franklin Watts
An imprint of
Hachette Children's Group
Part of The Watts Publishing Group
Carmelite House
50 Victoria Embankment
London EC4Y 0DZ

An Hachette UK Company
www.hachette.co.uk
www.franklinwatts.co.uk

Contents

Football – but not as we know it!   4

Football's thug-like beginnings   6

Football: worldwide fun   8

Breaking the rules   10

The best names in the game   12

Extreme fans   14

Knockout competition   16

Football's greatest upsets   18

Weird World Cup   20

Football extremes   22

Crazy keepers   24

Goals, glorious goals   26

It's a funny old game   28

Football quiz   30
Glossary   31
Index   32

Words in **bold** are in the glossary.

F⚽tball – but not as we know it!

It started out as just another game. It ended as the most bizarre international football match ever played!

Barbados v. Grenada

To qualify for the Caribbean Cup, Barbados needed to beat Grenada by two goals. Approaching full-time, they were 2-0 ahead and everything was going smoothly. Then, with just seven minutes to play, Grenada scored! Barbados had 420 seconds to grab another goal!

Usually, players get really upset about scoring an own goal.

Or maybe not …

… if the match was drawn, it would go to **extra time**. And the tournament rules said that extra-time goals counted double.

Barbados scored an own goal on purpose, making the score 2-2. Extra time beckoned. All Barbados needed was a golden goal in extra time. That would give them a 4-2 victory!

Going for (own) goals

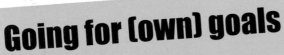

In 1998, Indonesia's goalkeeper kicked the ball into his own net to lose against Thailand. Both teams wanted to avoid meeting **favourites** Vietnam in the next match of the ASEAN (Association of Southeast Asian Nations) championship, and started attacking their own goal to lose the game. The guilty goalie was banned for life.

Any goal will do

For Grenada it didn't matter if they won, or lost by just one goal – they would still get into the Caribbean Cup. So as the clock ticked towards full time, Grenada's players needed to score… in EITHER goal. Barbados desperately defended … at BOTH ends of the pitch.

Barbados managed to stop Grenada scoring, then won the game in extra time. Grenada's coach said that whoever came up with the rules that led to this goofy game must be mad.

Strange – but true

If you told that story about your weekend match, no one would believe you. But like the story, everything in this book is true – however unbelievable it may seem.

Question & Answer

HANG ON, ISN'T THAT OUR GOAL?

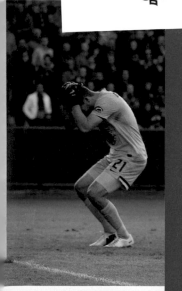

Q. What was amazing about Stan van den Buys' three goals for Belgian side Anderlecht in their win over Germinal Ekeren in January 1995?

A. Stan was playing for Germinal Ekeren and they were all own goals!

 You win some, you lose some: here Anderlecht benefit from an own goal scored by Thomas Meunier of Club Brugge.

F⚽️otball's thug-like beginnings

Today, football is sometimes called 'the beautiful game'. But when the earliest versions of football started to be played, no one would have called it that!

Fatal football

One of the first ever football reports, from England in 1280, tells how a player died after 'running against an opponent's dagger'!

A game of medieval-rules football being played in 2003.

Back then football was so violent that several rulers tried to ban the game altogether. In fact, the Mayor of London got so sick of the violence and damage caused by football matches, he banned them in the city.

Whole villages played one another, and there could be hundreds of players all chasing after the 'ball' (which was actually an inflated pig's bladder). There were few rules and no referees, so there wasn't really any such thing as a **foul**. Punching and kicking your opponent were considered part of the game. As a result, cuts, bruises, broken bones, internal injuries and deaths were all common.

The arrival of rules

By the 1600s, football had spread from the villages to Britain's **public schools**. Rules began to develop. Some matches even had referees! Then, in 1863, the Football Association (the FA) was formed in England. It was football's first governing body.

 By the 1920s, teams like this Chinese one were wearing very smart kit – even the coaches!

Wartime women's football

During the First World War (1914–18) women began working in factories, doing the jobs of men who were away fighting. The women also formed football teams. Their matches drew huge crowds – during and after the war. In 1920, 53,000 fans watched a women's match at Everton's ground. The biggest crowd to watch Everton's men's team that year was only 39,000.

Then, in 1921, the men of the FA decided women should be banned from playing in public. It said the sport was 'unsuitable' for females. Amazingly, this ban was only finally lifted in 1971.

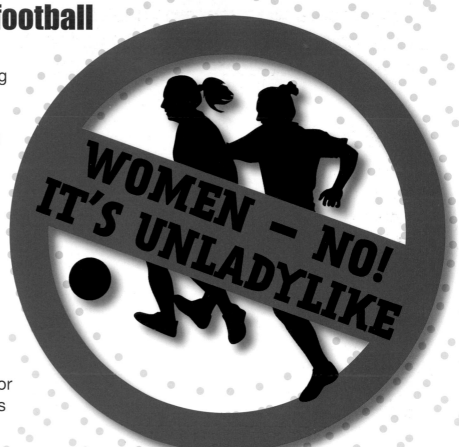

WOMEN – NO! IT'S UNLADYLIKE

WHAT DO YOU MEAN YOU'VE NEVER HEARD OF ... LILY PARR?

LILY PARR WAS THE FIRST FEMALE FOOTBALL SUPERSTAR!

SHE PLAYED FOR DICK KERR'S LADIES, FROM PRESTON. THE LADIES WERE THE FIRST WOMEN TO PLAY IN SHORTS. PARR WAS A *PROFESSIONAL* FOOTBALLER – AND AS SHE SMOKED, PART OF HER WAGES WAS PAID IN CIGARETTES!

F⚽⚽tball: worldwide fun

Most people think football was invented in England. (Well, most English people do, anyway.) But that may not be the whole story …

ANYONE FANCY A KICKABOUT?

Ancient football

Ancient Greeks and Romans both played games where teams had to get a ball to the opposition's end of the pitch. And in China from CE 100, *tsu'chu* involved trying to kick a leather ball into a goal just 40 cm across. Worse still, you could only shoot while being tackled. Games that involve kicking a ball around were also popular in other places – hundreds of years before English villagers started chasing pig bladders around.

⚽ In ancient China, soldiers used a football-like game for training.

The first international

By the late 1800s, football was really taking off. In 1872, the first ever international match was played. It was England v. Scotland. The teams played with extremely attacking **formations**: England 1-1-8 (one defender, one midfielder, eight attackers), Scotland 2-2-6!

Scotland v England, 1872. Nice hats!

England alone

Soon, it was not only England that had a football association. Scotland's had formed in 1873 and Wales's in 1876. But when a letter arrived from the Netherlands asking how to form an association, the English took two months to even reply. When **FIFA** was formed in 1904, England did not become a member. (The Netherlands did.) The English also didn't join in with the World Cup until 1950 – by which time it had already been taking place for 20 years!

Q. Who did mighty Brazil play their first ever match against?

A. Tiny Exeter City! Exeter had been chosen as a typical English team to go and play in Argentina. On their way home they played a few matches in Brazil – including one against 'Brazil', made up of the best players from Rio de Janeiro and São Paulo.

Scottish flag

Welsh flag

Dutch flag

Breaking the rules

Like most sportspeople, footballers are very competitive. They push the rules to the limits – and sometimes beyond.

Foot er, handball?

In football, you definitely do NOT use your hands to move the ball. But three of the most famous cheaters ever did just that – and two of them got away with it!

3rd Bruna

2011: In the Women's World Cup, Equatorial Guinea defender Bruna catches the ball in the penalty area, holds on to it for a couple of seconds, then drops it. Amazingly, the referee fails to notice and play continues. Fortunately, Australia still win 3–2.

2nd Diego Maradona

1986: Diego Maradona of Argentina handballs a goal past England in the World Cup quarter-final. The officials fail to spot it and the 'goal' helps knock England out.

Watch it here! ➤ https://tinyurl.com/pssaf8x

1st Luis Suárez

2010: Luis Suárez of Uruguay handballs to save a certain goal by Ghana in the World Cup quarter-final. He's sent off – but Ghana miss the resulting penalty and Uruguay still win.

Watch it here! ➤ https://tinyurl.com/z4fsvnx

True or False?

In 2016, Swedish footballer Adam Lindin Ljungkvist was sent off for farting.

True! Suspiciously, Ljungkvist said afterwards, "Maybe [the referee] thought I farted in my hand and threw the fart at him. But I did not." Now that is foul!

Match postponed!

Football matches sometimes have to be stopped, for example because of the weather or crowd trouble. Here are three of football's most unusual stoppages:

The world's longest match?

In 2004, Real Madrid were drawing 1–1 in a La Liga match with Real Sociedad with six minutes to play. Then there was a **bomb scare** and everyone left the stadium. The teams came back to play the last few minutes 24 days later. Madrid finally won 2–1.

The most postponed match?

1979 was a cold winter in Scotland. Inverness Thistle were due to play Falkirk, but the ground was frozen and the game was postponed. Then it was postponed again … and again … and again. In total, the game was postponed 29 times before things warmed up.

WEEEEEEE!

Bees stop play

A match in Brazil stopped before it had even started in 2013: a huge swarm of bees set up home on the **crossbar**! The match finally kicked off after the fire brigade came and took the bees away in a plastic sack.

Watch it here! ▶ https://tinyurl.com/k7osw6a

The best names in the game

The first modern football club was founded in Sheffield, England, in 1857. It was three years before another club formed and Sheffield FC could play their first official match!

Team titles that trip off the tongue

Since then, thousands of clubs have formed. And one or two of them have gone out of their way to come up with a memorable name …

Botswana

Name: Botswana Meat Commission
Country: Botswana (obviously…)

Botswana's football fans have some great team names to choose from, including the Naughty Boys. Best ever, though, has to be Botswana Meat Commission.

Bolivia

Name: The Strongest
Country: Bolivia

In the 1930s, players from this team fought in a war against neighbouring Paraguay. They were so fierce that one of the battles was actually named after them. Talk about living up to your name!

Name: Young Boys of Bern
Country: Switzerland

Swiss clubs have some great names ('Grasshoppers Zurich', anyone?). The Young Boys chose their name to distinguish themselves from Basel Old Boys and Bern Football Club.

Switzerland

Name: Hamilton Academical
Country: Scotland

Despite what you might think, Academical is not a team you only get into by being a bit of a boffin. The club was originally formed by players from the Hamilton Academy school, hence its odd name.

DREADFUL!

Name: Tottenham Hotspur
Country: England

Hotspur? What kind of name is that for a club? It actually comes from an old word for a fierce person, the kind of knight who would ride his horse with 'hot spurs'.

CHARGE!

Name: House of Dread
Country: Trinidad

In a country littered with great team names (Boss FC, Defence Force, Joe Public FC), surely House of Dread has the most intimidating one of all?

True or False?

Sheffield Wednesday got their name from the day they played their matches.

True! They were originally called the Wednesday Football Club, to show they were different from the Wednesday Cricket Club. That changed to Sheffield Wednesday in 1929.

Extreme fans

Football is famous for its passionate fans. In fact, the fans are sometimes SO passionate that they seem a bit bonkers (unless you are a fan yourself).

True or False?

Manchester City fans stole their goal celebration from Poland.

True! When the team scores, the fans turn their backs to the pitch, put their arms round each other's shoulders, and jump up and down. It is known as 'the Poznań' because the first fans to use it were from the Polish club Lech Poznań.

There are always one or two who don't get the message ... Most of Poznań's fans celebrate a goal against Warsaw in the Polish Cup Final.

Curse of the black cats

One of the most famous rivalries in football is between two sides from Argentina, Racing Club and Independiente. In 1967, a group of Independiente fans decided to put a curse on their rivals. They snuck into the stadium and buried the dead bodies of seven black cats.

Racing's team started to do worse and worse. Word of the curse got round. Six of the cats were unearthed, but Racing kept doing badly until the last cat was finally found in 2001. That year, Racing won the league title – for the first time since 1966.

Four famous rivalries

These are four cities whose fans have some of the most famous rivalries in football:

 ## 4th London

Arsenal v. Tottenham

These clubs from roughly the same area of London have disliked each other for so long, no one really remembers the reason why.

3rd Buenos Aires

Boca Juniors v. River Plate

Boca come from the poor docks area of Buenos Aires, River Plate from wealthy Núñez. Of course they don't like each other!

1st Glasgow

Celtic v. Rangers

Celtic's fans come mainly from the city's Catholic population, and Rangers' fans are mostly Protestant.

 ## 2nd Rome, Italy

Lazio v. Roma

A bitter rivalry since the 1930s. Roma fans think of themselves as city slickers, while Lazio are country **bumpkins**. Lazio don't agree.

Knockout competition

Normally, big clubs play other big clubs, and small clubs play other small ones. In a **knockout competition**, though, that is not always the case.

Embarrassing defeats

Once in a while a knockout competition throws up a terrible mismatch. Weirdly, the worst two ever were both in the Scottish Cup. Even weirder, the matches happened on the exact same day in 1885.

First Arbroath played Bon Accord. Bon Accord were dreadful. The Arbroath goalkeeper never touched the ball, and was so bored he spent part of the match standing under a spectator's umbrella. The Bon Accord goalie WAS kept busy – picking the ball from the back of the net. Arbroath eventually won 36-0 (and that was with seven goals **disallowed**).

36 : 0
Arbroath   **Bon Accord**

35 : 0
Dundee Harp   **Aberdeen Rovers**

Meanwhile 30 km away, Dundee Harp were thrashing Aberdeen Rovers 35-0. The score in this game may actually have been higher. The referee thought Dundee had scored 37 – but Aberdeen said no, it was 35. The ref admitted that with so many goals, he might have miscounted!

Stolen prize

In 1966 the biggest prize in football, the World Cup (then called the Jules Rimet Trophy), was stolen in England. The FA, who were meant to have been looking after it, got a ransom note. Pay £15,000 or the golden trophy gets melted down! A man was arrested trying to collect the **ransom**, but the cup was not recovered. It WAS eventually found at the side of the road – by a dog called Pickles.

Pickles became a hero. He got a medal and a year's supply of dog food as a reward. He was even invited to the World Cup winner's dinner … where Pickles showed how unimpressed he was by weeing on one of the entrance doors.

YOU CALL!

Pickles the dog, his owner, and the spot where Pickles found the World Cup.

True or False?

Italy won the 1968 European Championships due to the toss of a coin.

True! Well, mostly true. Italy's semi-final against the **USSR** ended 0–0, so the teams tossed a coin to see who went to the final. Italy won.

F⚽⚽tball's greatest upsets

Usually in football, the big team beats the little one. Usually… but not always. In the history of the game, there have been some amazing upsets.

✹ Leicester win the league ✹

At the start of the 2015–16 Premier League season, the odds on Leicester City winning the league were 5,000/1. This meant it was thought more likely that …

✦ **Simon Cowell would be the next prime minister (500/1).**

✦ **Prime Minister David Cameron would become Aston Villa manager (2,500/1).**

✦ **Sir Alex Ferguson would win 'Strictly Come Dancing' (1,000/1).**

Amazingly, (even to their fans), Leicester DID win the league!

IF YOU THINK **THIS** IS UNLIKELY …

True or False?

Denmark won Euro 1992 – even though they didn't even qualify.

The answer is true! In qualifying, Denmark had missed out to **Yugoslavia**. But weeks before the tournament started, the civil war in Yugoslavia led to it's team being withdrawn. Denmark took their place, and went on to win.

Four massive upsets

Denmark winning Euro 92 (see True or False) was a massive shock. It's far from the only amazing one in football – here are four more:

① Greece win Euro 2004

At the start, Greece had never won a match in a big international tournament. By the end, they had won the whole competition, beating hosts Portugal 1-0 in the final.

Watch it here! ➤ Greece's winning goal: https://tinyurl.com/hk6bz7o

② Faroe Islands beat Austria. And Greece – twice

In 1990, in their first ever international match, the tiny Faroe Islands beat Austria 1-0. They were at it again in 2014. The islanders (ranked 187th in the world) beat Greece (ranked 18th) 1-0. Then in 2015 they beat Greece AGAIN, this time 2-1!

③ USA beat England in 1950

In 1950, England was probably the world's best team. So it came as a mighty shock when they lost their second ever World Cup match 1-0, to a team of part-timers from the USA.

Watch it here! ➤ The story of England's shock defeat: https://tinyurl.com/ztkzrk3

④ Iceland beat England in 2016

By 2016, England losing no longer really counted as a surprise. Iceland definitely thought they could win, even with a population roughly 0.6 per cent as big as England's and no professional clubs. And they did, 2-1.

England: Population approximately 53 million

Iceland: Population approximately 300,000

Weird World Cup

The World Cup is the biggest competition in football. It can take years just to qualify. When teams finally make it, the pressure sometimes causes some pretty strange behaviour.

US trainer knocks himself out

The strangeness started at the first World Cup in 1930. The US trainer ran on to argue with the ref. As he got there, he dropped the medical bag he had been holding. A bottle of **chloroform** inside broke – and the trainer fell to the ground unconscious.

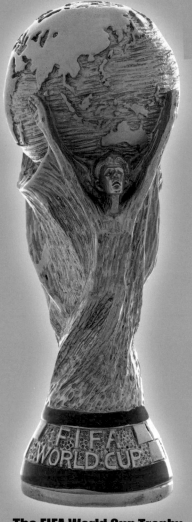

The FIFA World Cup Trophy

Argentina goalie wees on pitch

Argentina's goalkeeper at the 1990 World Cup apparently did a little wee on the pitch when he had to face a penalty. He claimed to have done this because he needed to during the quarter-finals, then kept doing it for luck. 'I was very subtle,' he said, 'nobody complained'.

GOOD JOB THIS ISN'T THE WORLD CUP...

Zaire defender panics

In 1974, the team from Zaire had already lost 9-0 to Yugoslavia. Zaire's violent ruler, President Mobutu, sent a message:

IF YOU LOSE 4-0 OR WORSE, DO NOT COME HOME.

The problem was, the next match was against world champions Brazil! The Zaire players made a mighty effort. With five minutes to play, the score was 3-0.

Then Brazil got a free kick in a scoring position. The referee blew his whistle for Brazil to take the kick – and in a panic, the Zaire defender Mwepu Ilunga raced forward and booted the ball as far down the pitch as he could. He got a yellow card. The free kick was taken again, Brazil failed to score, and the Zaire players were able to go home.

Watch it here! ▶ https://tinyurl.com/jlffv3f

WORLD CUP PREDICTIONS HERE!

True or False?

An octopus correctly predicted the 2010 World Cup results.

True! Paul the Octopus lived in an aquarium in Germany. He correctly predicted the result of all seven of Germany's matches.

Paul also correctly predicted the result of the final, Spain v. Netherlands, by choosing for his dinner a mussel from a box with a Spanish flag on it.

F⚽⚽tball extremes

Every fan knows that football is a game of extreme emotions, from joy to **despondency**. And it's not only the emotions that can be extreme.

⚽ Cristiano Ronaldo, said to be the world's best-paid footballer. Ronaldo apparently took home £365,000 a week in 2016-17.

£££££££ Extreme money £££££££

In 1922, the brilliantly named Sydney Puddlefoot joined Falkirk. The Scottish club paid a world-record **transfer fee** of ... £5,000. Fast forward to 2016. Manchester United set a new record of ... £89 million for Paul Pogba. That's 17,800 times as much as Puddlefoot!

Transfer fees are not the only football cost that has gone up. In 1957, an England international player earned about £1,677 a year. The equivalent today is about £75,000. Today's top England players still earn about that much – but every WEEK!

1957 wages

2017 wages

CA$H

⚽ By 2017, an England player could expect to earn around 50 times as much as one from 60 years earlier.

WHAT DO YOU MEAN YOU'VE NEVER HEARD OF... ERIC CANTONA?

CANTONA WAS ONE OF THE MOST ECCENTRIC FOOTBALLERS EVER!

A BRILLIANT FORWARD PLAYER, CANTONA WAS ONCE BANNED FOR EIGHT MONTHS AFTER KUNG-FU KICKING AN OPPOSING FAN. CANTONA'S COMMENT TO THE PRESS?

'WHEN THE SEAGULLS FOLLOW THE TRAWLER, IT'S BECAUSE THEY THINK SARDINES WILL BE THROWN INTO THE SEA. THANK YOU VERY MUCH.'

Extreme behaviour

Away from the pitch, footballers sometimes behave quite oddly:

Mario Balotelli of Italy admits he 'does strange things'. Such as: driving into a women's prison to look around; telling a police officer that he had £5,000 in his car 'because I am rich'; and setting fire to his house with fireworks.

Wayne Rooney of England hates being alone, and sometimes turns on the hairdryer in hotel rooms to pretend there's someone else there.

At the 1998 World Cup, Laurent Blanc of France always kissed the goalie's shaved head before kick-off for luck. And the whole team listened to Gloria Gaynor's 'I Will Survive' the night before every game.

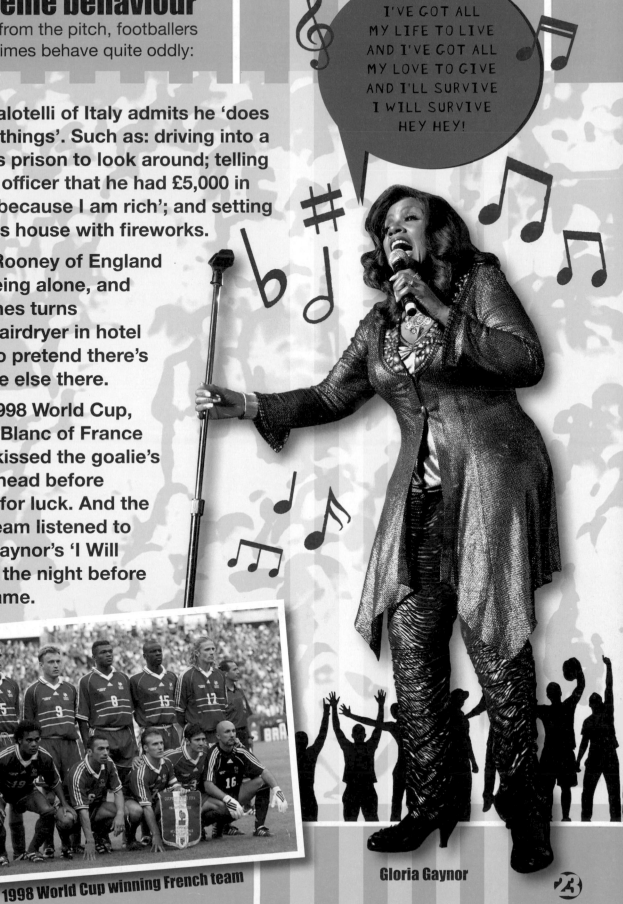

I'VE GOT ALL MY LIFE TO LIVE AND I'VE GOT ALL MY LOVE TO GIVE AND I'LL SURVIVE I WILL SURVIVE HEY HEY!

Gloria Gaynor

1998 World Cup winning French team

Crazy keepers

Goalkeepers are often said to be a bit crazy: maybe it's all that time standing on their own? The keepers covered here were certainly a bit out there.

True or False

José Chilavert of Paraguay is the only keeper to score a hat trick.

False! But sort of true, too. Chilavert scored a **hat trick** of penalties while playing as a goalie. Other keepers have scored hat tricks, but while playing as emergency **outfield** players. And one or two hat-trick strikers have finished matches in goal.

The amazing Hope Solo

Hope Solo of the USA is one of the best international keepers ever. She once went 55 international matches in a row without letting in a SINGLE goal! In total, by 2016 Solo had stopped the opposition scoring in 102 games.

 Hope Solo gets her 148th cap for the USA.

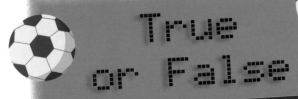

Unlucky Santi

OUCH!

Spain's Santiago Canizares was on his way to the 2002 World Cup when he dropped a bottle of aftershave. The bottle broke, Canizares trod on a bit of glass and cut a tendon in his foot. The unlucky keeper had to stay at home.

Canizares is not the only goalie to be injured in strange circumstances:

★ England's David James hurt his back reaching for a TV remote, and injured his shoulder trying to catch a giant carp.

WOOF!

★ Southampton's Dave Beasant was injured dropping a bottle of salad cream on his foot.

SALAD CREAM

★ Chic Brodie of Brentford broke his knee falling over a dog that ran onto the pitch (and stole the ball).

WHAT DO YOU MEAN YOU'VE NEVER HEARD OF... RENÉ HIGUITA?

HE HAD THE CRAZIEST PASS OUT OF DEFENCE EVER! WHEN THE BALL CAME TOWARDS HIM, HIGUITA WOULD LINE IT UP, LEAP FORWARD AND ARCH HIS BACK LIKE A SCORPION. THEN HE WOULD KICK THE BALL AWAY WITH HIS HEELS. HIGUITA'S BUCCANEERING STYLE OF PLAY, LEAVING HIS GOAL FAR BEHIND, EARNED HIM THE NICKNAME 'EL LOCO' — THE MADMAN.

  **Watch it here!** El loco's craziest moments at https://tinyurl.com/ogsxdww

25

Goals, glorious goals

Football is a complicated game with a simple aim: score more goals than the other team.
Of course, not all goals are the same.

Strange goals

3 In a 2009 match against Liverpool, Darren Bent's shot rocketed into a beachball that had been thrown on the pitch. The football went right, the beachball went left and the goalkeeper didn't know which way to turn. **GOAL** to Bent's Sunderland! To make it worse, the beachball had been thrown on the pitch by a Liverpool fan.

Watch it here! https://tinyurl.com/z7wed6y

2 Every goalkeeper dreams of saving a penalty in a crucial game. When Morocco's Khalid Askri thought he'd done exactly that, he ran off to celebrate. Unfortunately, the spinning ball then gently rolled into the net. **Not saved after all!** Lesson: always make sure you kick the ball clear before you start celebrating.

Watch it here! https://tinyurl.com/hugluy8

1 In 2011, Festus Baise scored one of the best goals ever in the Hong Kong first division. As the ball was crossed, he leapt in the air and arched his back to kick the ball. It sailed high into the air and into the corner of the net … his own team's net. **Own goal!** Fortunately his team went on to win 3-2.

Watch it here! https://tinyurl.com/h5mq92a

Top goals

Ask seven football fans to name the best goal ever, and you get seven different answers.

But here is a top three for discussion:

BALL … EAT NET!

Corner

David Beckham, LA Galaxy v. Chicago Fire, 2011
Even Beckham can't have thought this would work. His low-flying corner kick swung in and went straight into the net. The Chicago Fire's goalkeeper must have found it hard to get to sleep that night.

Watch it here! ▶ https://tinyurl.com/j52jlg5

David Beckham of LA Galaxy lines up one of his famous dead-ball **kicks**.

Paul Gascoigne celebrates with his teammates after his wonder goal against Scotland.

Volley

Paul Gascoigne, England v. Scotland, 1996
As the ball comes to him, England's Gascoigne volleys it gently over his own shoulder and the closing defender. He turns and meets it on the way down, unleashing a second volley – an absolute rocket, which flies into the net.

Watch it here! ▶ https://tinyurl.com/hca3azl

Watch it here! ▶ https://tinyurl.com/jqnqazt

Free kick

Roberto Carlos, Brazil v. France, 1997
Brazil's Carlos once scored with a free kick from the centre circle. This one was closer to the goal, but not much. Carlos took a 15-m run-up and belted it. The ball swerved and swirled, and travelled so fast all the French could do was watch, stunned, as it flew into the net.

It's a funny old game

After all that strangeness you might think you have heard every odd footballing fact. But football has lots more random stories to tell. Here are just a few:

Victories and defeats

Sometimes, a team wins big. Not big like Spurs' 9–1 **thrashing** of Wigan in 2009 – WAY bigger than that. The biggest score in league football is said to have been 149–0, at a game in Madagascar.

149 : 0

Adema-SO   l'Emyrne

In international football, the record for the biggest win is held by Australia, who beat American Samoa 31-0 in 2001. American Samoa included three 15-year-olds, and as the English commentator Alan Hansen famously said, "You can't win anything with kids."

Mind you, Hansen had been talking about young Manchester United players – who then won the Premier League and FA Cup. So maybe that wasn't the problem!

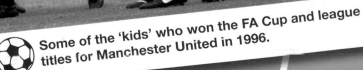
Some of the 'kids' who won the FA Cup and league titles for Manchester United in 1996.

It's tough at the top

Because football managers are in charge of the team, they often lose their job if the team plays badly. Some last longer than others.

 Leroy Rosenior was in charge of Torquay United for a record-setting TEN MINUTES before the club's new owners sacked him, in 2007.

Get new job

Leave new job

JUNE 1984

1	2	3	4	5	6
7	8	9	10	11	12
13	14	15	16	17	18
19	20	21	22	23	24
25	26	27	28	29	30

Rosenior broke the record of Dave Bassett, who was in charge of Crystal Palace for just four days in 1984.

 Sam Allardyce set a new record for England when he was sacked after 67 days in charge. Mind you, he also became the country's most successful manager, with a 100 per cent winning record in his single match in charge.

DOH!

England's most successful manager?

Football quiz

2 Which player hand-balled England out of the 1986 World Cup?

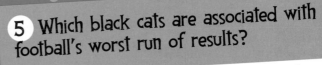

a. David Beckham, who got sent off and left England without their best penalty taker
b. The Argentina goalkeeper Nery Pumpido, who saved a brilliant shot from Gary Lineker
c. Argentina's Diego Maradona, who pushed the ball into the net while pretending to head it

1 Who found the stolen Jules Rimet Trophy in 1966?

a. London's Metropolitan Police
b. Private detectives hired by FIFA
c. It was never found
d. Pickles the dog

3 The Young Boys of Bern got their name ...

a. Because they were all under 21 when they played their first match, in 1898
b. To distinguish themselves from the Basel Old Boys
c. Because their manager's name was Franz Young

5 Which black cats are associated with football's worst run of results?

a. Sunderland FC, nicknamed the Black Cats, who once set an English Premier League record for scoring fewest points in a season
b. The black cats buried around the Racing Club stadium in Argentina, which led to a 34-year run of bad results
c. The black cat that ran across the pitch as Barcelona were playing Juventus, tripping up the referee and causing him to break his wrist

4 When did England's World Cup campaigns first start to go wrong?

a. What do you mean, 'go wrong'?
b. In the team's first-ever World Cup, in 1950, when England lost their second match 1-0 to USA
c. In 1930, when England decided not to even bother going to the World Cup

6 Who is England's most successful manager?

a. Sam Allardyce
b. Alf Ramsey
c. Fabio Capello
d. Walter Winterbottom

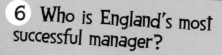

Glossary

bomb scare false information to say that a bomb has been left somewhere and is going to explode

bumpkin person from the countryside thought to be simple

cap term for a player's appearance (not including substitute appearances) in an international game

chloroform liquid chemicals that, when smelled, can make you unconscious

crossbar long, horizontal bar of a goal

dead ball ball that is not moving, such as a ball put down for a goal kick, corner, free kick or penalty

despondency feeling unhappy and without hope

disallow not count; for example, a goal scored by fouling the goalkeeper would not count

extra time time added to a football match when the score is equal, so that the teams have a chance to win

favourite team or person expected to win

FIFA short for Fédération Internationale de Football Association, the organisation in charge of football around the world

formation positions taken by outfield players on a pitch. For example, a team with four defenders, four midfielders and two strikers would be playing in a 4-4-2 formation

foul play that is not allowed in the rules of football, including dangerous or violent tackles

hat trick three goals for the same person all scored in the same match

knockout competition sports contest in which being beaten means leaving the contest (or being 'knocked out')

medieval to do with the Middle Ages, which lasted from about CE 400 to CE 1400.

outfield in football, an outfield player is everyone except the goalkeeper

professional paid; a professional footballer is paid to play

public school in the UK, a public school is a school that charges fees. Most public schools are boarding schools

ransom demand for money to trigger the release of something precious

sacked losing your job

thrash beaten by an embarrassingly large score

transfer fee money paid to a football club in exchange for one of their players

USSR country that existed from 1922 to 1991. It then broke up into, among other countries, Armenia, Georgia, Russia and Ukraine

Yugoslavia country that existed between 1929 and 1990, when it split up and became Bosnia-Herzegovina, Croatia, Macedonia, Montenegro, Serbia and Slovenia

Index

Allardyce, Sam 29
Askri, Khalid 26

Baise, Festus 26
Balotelli, Mario 23
Beasant, Dave 25
Beckham, David 27
Bent, Darren 26
Blanc, Laurent 23
Brodie, Chic 25
Bruna 10
Buys, Stan van den 5

Canizares, Santiago 25
Cantona, Eric 22
Caribbean Cup 4–5
Carlos, Roberto 27
Chilavert, José 24
China, ancient 8
competitions,
    knockout 16

Dick Kerr's Ladies 7

European
    Championships 17–19

fans 12, 14–15
fees, transfer 22
FIFA 9, 20
First World War 7
Football Association
    (FA) 6–7, 17, 28
football,
    medieval 6
    women's 7, 10, 24

Gascoigne, Paul 27
goalkeepers 4, 16, 20,
    23–27

goals,
    best ever 27
    own goals 4–5, 26

handball 10
Higuita, Rene 25

James, David 25

Ljungkvist, Adam Lindin
    10

managers, football 29
Maradona, Diego 10

Parr, Lily 7
Paul the Octopus 21
Pickles 17
Pogba, Paul 22
Premier League 18, 28
Puddlefoot, Sydney 22

Roberto, Carlos 27
Ronaldo, Cristiano 22
Rooney, Wayne 23
Rosenior, Leroy 29

Scottish Cup 16
Solo, Hope 24
stoppages, unusual 11
Suárez, Luis 10

teams
    Aberdeen Rovers 16
    American Samoa 28
    Arbroath 16
    Argentina 10, 20, 22
    Arsenal 15
    Austria 19
    Australia 10, 28

teams (continued)
    Barbados 4–5
    Boca Junior 15
    Bon Accord 16
    Botswana Meat
     Commission 12
    Brazil 9; 21, 27
    Celtic 15
    Denmark 18–19
    Dundee Harp 16
    England 9, 10, 19, 22,
     25, 27, 29
    Equatorial Guinea 10
    Everton 7
    Exeter City 9
    Falkirk 11, 22
    Faroe Islands 19
    France 23, 27
    Germany 21
    Ghana 10
    Greece 19
    Grenada 4–5
    Hamilton Academical
     13
    House of Dread 13
    Iceland 19
    Independiente 14
    Indonesia 4
    Inverness Thistle 11
    Italy 17
    LA Galaxy 27
    Lazio 15
    Leicester City 18
    Liverpool 26
    Manchester City 14
    Manchester United
     22, 28
    Netherlands 9, 21
    Paraguay 24
    Portugal 19

teams (continued)
    Racing Club 14
    Rangers 15
    Real Madrid 11
    Real Sociedad 11
    River Plate 15
    Roma 15
    Scotland 9, 27
    Sheffield FC 12
    Sheffield Wednesday
     13
    Southampton 25
    Spain 21
    Sunderland 26
    Thailand 4
    The Strongest 12
    Tottenham Hotspur
     13, 15
    Uruguay 10
    USA 19, 24
    USSR 17
    Vietnam 4
    Wales 9
    Young Boys of Bern
     12
    Yugoslavia 18, 21
    Zaire 21

World Cup 9, 10, 17,
    19–21, 23, 25